AF228665

# Cristiano Ronaldo

# Cristiano Ronaldo

## Soccer's Greatest Scorer

Leslie Holleran

LERNER PUBLICATIONS ◆ MINNEAPOLIS

Lerner Publications Company
An imprint of Lerner Publishing Group, Inc.
241 First Avenue North
Minneapolis, MN 55401 USA

For reading levels and more information, look up this title at www.lernerbooks.com.

Main body text set in Rotis Serif Std 55 Regular. Typeface provided by Adobe Systems.

**Editor:** Ashley Kuehl **Designer:** Lauren Cooper **Photo Editor:** Lucien Brinkley
**Lerner team:** Sue Marquis


**Library of Congress Cataloging-in-Publication Data**

Names: Holleran, Leslie, author.
Title: Cristiano Ronaldo : soccer's greatest scorer / Leslie Holleran.
Description: Minneapolis : Lerner Publications , 2025. | Series: Gateway biographies | Includes bibliographical references and index. | Audience: Ages 9–14 | Audience: Grades 4–6 | Summary: "Cristiano Ronaldo's mastery of the soccer field overshadows his fashion and charitable empires. Readers will explore Ronaldo's journey to superstardom and find out how he became one of the world's most popular athletes"– Provided by publisher.
Identifiers: LCCN 2024023100 (print) | LCCN 2024023101 (ebook) | ISBN 9798765649169 (library binding) | ISBN 9798765661789 (paperback) | ISBN 9798765654835 (epub)
Subjects: LCSH: Ronaldo, Cristiano, 1985– | Soccer players–Portugal–Biography–Juvenile literature.
Classification: LCC GV942.7.R626 H65 2025  (print) | LCC GV942.7.R626  (ebook) | DDC 796.334092 [B]–dc23/eng/20240530

LC record available at https://lccn.loc.gov/2024023100
LC ebook record available at https://lccn.loc.gov/2024023101

Manufactured in the United States of America
2-1012602-53496-1/21/2026

# TABLE OF CONTENTS

Cristiano Ronaldo in 2024

When opposing fans give a player a standing ovation, something remarkable must have occurred.

Real Madrid forward Cristiano Ronaldo awed Juventus fans during a 2018 UEFA Champions League quarterfinal. In the game's final 30 minutes, teammate Dani Carvajal floated a cross, a type of pass, toward the goal. Ronaldo leaped off the ground like a superhero. He made a stunning bicycle kick with his right leg. The ball flew past Juventus's goalie Gianluigi Buffon and into the bottom left corner of the net. Goal! Juventus fans got to their feet, and the stadium roared with applause.

The sensational goal was the work of a five-time Ballon d'Or (Golden Ball) winner at the top of his game.

Ronaldo's bicycle kick in the 2018 UEFA Champions League quarterfinal helped his team win the match.

Ronaldo has since called it his all-time favorite goal. Real Madrid won the match with Juventus 3–0 and went on to win the Champions League for the third straight year. Ronaldo led the league in total goals scored with over 100. These were just a few of Ronaldo's accomplishments in 2018.

As a young child, Ronaldo played soccer in the streets of Madeira, a Portuguese island. His beloved sport has since taken him around the world. He has played with five different clubs in as many countries and represented Portugal in international tournaments, including the World Cup.

As a child, Cristiano lived in Funchal, Portugal.

## LITTLE BEE

Cristiano Ronaldo dos Santos Aveiro was born on February 5, 1985, in Funchal, Portugal. Funchal is the capital of Madeira. The subtropical Madeira Islands are 600 miles (965 km) southwest of mainland Portugal in the Atlantic Ocean.

Cristiano was the fourth child of José Dinis Aveiro and Maria Dolores dos Santos Aveiro. He was also their second son. Cristiano's brother, Hugo, was their firstborn child. Sisters Elma and Cátia came next. Cristiano was born nine years after Cátia.

Cristiano at age two

Cristiano's aunt, his mother's sister, suggested his first name. His parents chose his middle name, Ronaldo, for then US president Ronald Reagan.

His dad worked as a city gardener, and his mom was a cook. His dad also helped out as a kit man for the local soccer club, Andorinha. A kit man manages the team's equipment. Aveiro asked Andorinha's team captain, Fernão Sousa, to be Cristiano's godfather. Sousa had previously played for Nacional da Madeira, another local soccer club.

One Christmas Sousa gave Cristiano a remote-controlled car. But Cristiano preferred his soccer ball to the toy. He carried his ball everywhere he went and even slept with it. It was his best friend.

Cristiano played soccer in the street as a young child since there wasn't a neighborhood pitch. After school he'd grab a snack and then meet his friends. They used stones as goalposts and kept an eye out for traffic. When a car or bus came along, they removed the stones temporarily. Sometimes the ball landed in a neighbor's garden. If it was Mr. Agostinho's garden, he'd threaten to puncture the ball and talk to their mothers. Nevertheless, Cristiano and his friends played this way for years.

Cristiano, at around eight years old, in uniform for his Andorinha youth team

During elementary school, Cristiano's cousin Nuno, an Andorinha youth player, invited him to watch his team. Cristiano then joined the team at Nuno's suggestion. He won his first tournament trophy with their Andorinha team. Both his parents were happy that he was playing. They had always loved soccer. His dad and brother, Hugo, were fans of Portuguese team Benfica, while his mom adored their rival team, Sporting Lisbon.

Though Cristiano did fine in school, soccer (called football outside of the United States) came first for him. Sousa said, "When the other kids were studying, he would put his studies on the back seat in order to play football."

Cristiano demonstrated athletic talent early on. His first coach, Francisco Afonso, said, "He was fast, he was technically brilliant, and he played equally well with his left and right foot."

Because he was quick and always in motion, he earned the nickname abelinha. It's Portuguese for "little bee."

Cristiano desperately wanted to win his soccer matches. Losing brought him to tears. He cried so often that he earned another nickname: crybaby. He didn't want to compete against stronger teams. So, his dad got involved and gave him the guidance he needed. One day when Cristiano was hiding from a match, his father persuaded him to put on his uniform and go join his team. He told his son that only the weak give up.

# SPORTING CHANCE

Before long, word had spread around Madeira about Cristiano's soccer abilities. The two largest clubs on the island became interested in him.

Cristiano's godfather, Fernão Sousa, was then a youth coach at his former club Nacional. It was one of the teams interested in 10-year-old Cristiano. Sousa was delighted that the young player everyone was talking about was his godson. He wanted to take him from Andorinha to Nacional. Sousa told Cristiano's mother it would be a great move for him. They reached an agreement with Andorinha. Cristiano's first club got 20 soccer balls and two sets of uniforms in exchange.

This 2020 photo shows players from the Nacional club in Madeira, a team Cristiano played for as a child.

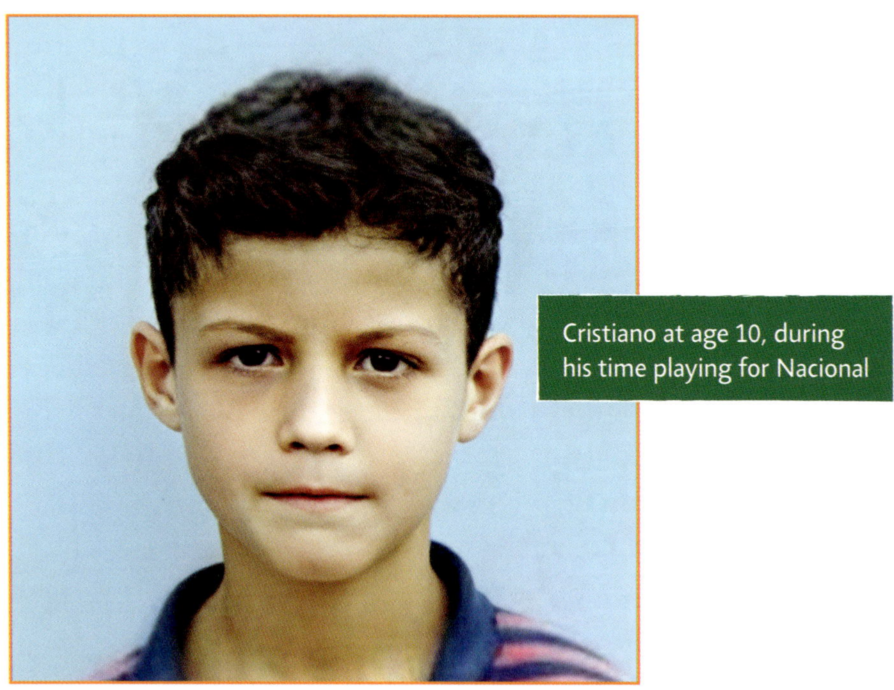

Cristiano at age 10, during his time playing for Nacional

Nacional was very pleased with their new player. His new coach, António Mendonça, said, "Street football had taught him how to avoid getting hit, sidestep the opponent, and face up to kids much bigger than he was." The only thing Nacional wanted to change about Cristiano was his weight. He was a bit skinny, so the coaches wanted him to eat more. He was still getting upset about losing, but his Nacional teammates put up with it. They were winning matches nine or 10 to zero thanks to him. At the age of 11, he helped Nacional win a regional title in the league for 10-to-12-year-olds.

Sousa soon stepped up to help Cristiano again. This time, he made a connection with Sporting Lisbon, a

Sporting Lisbon plays at Estádio José Alvalade, shown here.

professional club on the mainland. The club has a highly regarded school and an established scouting system for youth players. Cristiano earned a tryout in Lisbon. With his mom's approval, Cristiano went with Sousa to Sporting's facilities. It was Cristiano's first trip off Madeira. He was so nervous that he couldn't sleep the night before. The trial went well. Cristiano impressed both players and coaches. Sporting was ready to enroll him into its school.

In the late summer, Cristiano tearfully said goodbye to his family. He and his mom traveled together to Lisbon. He would begin training while continuing school. He also needed to adapt to living in a dormitory. At 12 years old, he was the dorm's youngest resident.

Cristiano's first year was an undeniable ordeal for him. On his first day of school, he arrived late because he couldn't find the building. Then, when he spoke, students laughed at him. He recalled, "My first day of school was terrible. . . . As soon as I spoke, the kids at the back of the room started laughing and making fun of my accent." Just as English sounds different depending on where someone is from, so does Portuguese. Cristiano had a heavy Madeiran accent. The embarrassment made him sweat.

## Ball Boy

Cristiano had a part-time job while he studied at Sporting's youth academy. He worked as a ball boy for Sporting's professional team. Ball boys were paid five euros ($5.36) per game, but it was the experience of being on the pitch with the team that meant the most to him. He said, "The money did not mean a thing when compared with the thrill of being down there . . . close to the players and with the opportunity of being able to play with the ball during the interval." After the matches, Cristiano and fellow ball boys pooled their earnings for a three-for-one pizza deal.

In the following days and weeks, Cristiano became homesick. He cried almost daily. Living independently from his family at such a young age felt unbearable. He wanted to give up his opportunity and return home. When he said that he had had enough, his mom flew to Lisbon to visit. She encouraged him not to quit. She also reminded him that soccer was his dream. If he wanted to make it come true, then his future depended on staying at Sporting.

Eventually, Cristiano's schoolmates stopped teasing him, and he made friends at the academy. With his family's help, he put his dream of becoming a professional soccer player first. After that, he was able to settle into his new life.

Ronaldo and his mother after a match in 2009

# DOGGED DETERMINATION

Cristiano wanted, more than anything, to excel at soccer. But he didn't feel the same about schoolwork. By the ninth grade, Sporting allowed him to discontinue his studies. His mother supported his decision.

He still hadn't developed physically at 14 years old. So, he chose to work out during his free time. But Sporting placed strict limits on weight training by youth academy players. Its approach was for them to develop without it. But Cristiano didn't want to wait any longer, so he went ahead and lifted weights anyway. He creatively sidestepped every barrier Sporting put in his way. Since he was seeing results, he wasn't going to stop. He said, "I got bigger and faster. And then I would walk onto the field—and the people who used to whisper, 'Yeah, but he's so skinny'? Now they would be looking at me like it was the end of the world."

Cristiano was also making progress toward his goal of becoming a professional. By the age of 16, he was one of the best players in the academy. He began practicing with the club's first, or top, team, and Sporting's coach László Bölöni had his eye on him. In 2002 Bölöni began working with him to prepare him for joining the team. To increase his effectiveness, Bölöni repositioned him on the wing. He also guided him in passing the ball more.

Bölöni promoted Cristiano to the first team ahead of the summer. He played in several friendly matches during the preseason. In an early August match against Spain's Real Betis, he scored his first goal. The match was in

Ronaldo (*right*) tries to block a shot by
Derlei from Portuguese team Porto in 2003.

overtime when Cristiano sealed Sporting's 3–2 victory.
He hustled down the field. Then, from the left wing, he
kicked the ball high and right. It landed perfectly inside
the goal. He celebrated the moment by blowing kisses into
the stands.

By October he'd made Sporting's starting lineup for the
first time. The team was playing a Portuguese SuperLiga
match versus Moreirense. Cristiano scored twice and
stole the spotlight from Sporting striker Mário Jardel,

a two-time Golden Boot winner. Cristiano was on the front cover of Portugal's *Record*, a sports newspaper, the next day. The headline read: "Phenomenon." His mom was at the game for this milestone in her son's career and nearly fainted.

By the end of his first season, he'd become a regular in Sporting's starting lineup. He played in 25 games with the first team, started in 11, scored five goals, and made five assists. In June he represented Portugal at an Under-20 tournament in Toulon, France. In the final, Portugal beat Italy 3–1 and won its third tournament trophy.

Ronaldo (*center*) with his mother and brother in 2014

Cristiano was starting his second season with Sporting on solid footing. He had also sparked interest from several top European clubs at the tournament. His agent, Jorge Mendes, was speaking with them behind the scenes.

## MANCHESTER'S NEW MAN

Sporting's preseason included a friendly match against England's Manchester United on August 6, 2003. The game marked the opening of Sporting's new stadium, Estádio José Alvalade.

Ronaldo was in top form that day and made a powerful impression on the United players. The England team had just flown back to Europe from the United States for the match. Defender John O'Shea said, "That's the last thing you need when jet-lagged—a young lad wanting to run at you time and again, going left, going right, twisting, turning, shooting every time he got within distance of the goal." By halftime, United's players were urging their coach, Alex Ferguson, to sign him. Though Ronaldo didn't score, he helped Sporting win 3–1.

What the United players didn't know then was that their club had been watching Ronaldo for some time. Furthermore, an agreement had already been reached among Manchester United, Sporting Lisbon, and Ronaldo's agent. Ronaldo was joining the Red Devils. It was his last match with Sporting. The transfer was kept under wraps to keep the media's attention on Sporting's new stadium. Ronaldo would leave for England two days later. Manchester's timeline surprised even Ronaldo. He had assumed he would play one more season with Sporting, but Ferguson was eager to have him on the team.

Ronaldo made his first appearance at Old Trafford, Manchester United's stadium, less than two weeks later. He received a standing ovation on taking the pitch. He was the first Portuguese player to sign with United.

Manchester United coach Alex Ferguson and Ronaldo in August 2003, during the week that Ronaldo agreed to join the team

# Maintaining Athletic Excellence

Ronaldo has shown a steadfast commitment to physical training ever since his days at Sporting's Academy. He worked with Mick Clegg, Manchester United's power development coach, to further develop his athleticism. Clegg said that Ronaldo invested "thousands and thousands of hours of [hard work] to turn himself into the perfect player." Ronaldo didn't let up when he went to Real Madrid. There he developed an all-encompassing program with fitness coach Valter Di Salvo. It covered everything—conditioning, nutrition, and sleep—and everything was tracked.

Ronaldo (*right*) trains with the Portuguese national team before the 2024 European Football Championship.

Unlike when he'd moved to Lisbon, Ronaldo had company this time. His mom, sister Cátia, cousin Nuno, and brother-in-law José relocated with him. Having their company prevented him from another serious bout of loneliness. And Cátia and José both spoke English, so they helped to translate. Ronaldo was learning the language with a tutor during his first few years in England. His goal was to be fluent by the World Cup in 2006.

The language wasn't the only difference between Portugal and England. Ronaldo also had to learn to drive on the left side of the road. The adjustment was tricky. He said, "I cannot help but smile when I recall the many [sidewalks] I mounted when I tried the new experience of driving on the left." He got used to that and to England's narrow streets within a few months.

Ronaldo finished strong in his first season. He then represented Portugal at UEFA Euro 2004, a competition among European men's national teams. He played with his childhood heroes Rui Costa and

Ronaldo in a 2004 UEFA European Football Championship match

Luís Figo. Figo was the Portuguese team captain. Ronaldo scored his first goal for Portugal during the first game against Greece. Portugal met Greece again in the final match and lost. It was a surprising upset—Greece had never before won a match at a major event.

The following summer, Ronaldo represented Portugal at the World Cup qualifiers in Russia. The night before his first game, Portugal's coach, Luiz Felipe Scolari, requested to meet with him. Scolari had some important, difficult news to relay. Ronaldo's father had died of liver failure at the London hospital where he was being treated.

Scolari offered him the opportunity to leave so he could be with his family. But Ronaldo didn't want to go yet. He wanted to play in the match first. He said, "I am going to play a game in honor of my father, I will play for him." And he did. He also wanted to score a goal for his dad, who had always encouraged Ronaldo from his earliest soccer days. The goal for his dad didn't happen at the qualifying match in Russia, but it did at the 2006 World Cup in Germany.

## UNFORGETTABLE SENSATION

In 2006 Portugal made it to the World Cup final 16 for the first time in 40 years. In the quarterfinals, the team faced England. Ronaldo went head-to-head with some of his United teammates, including Wayne Rooney and Gary Neville.

The Portugal national team before the 2006
World Cup quarterfinal match against England

The match ended in a draw, leading to a penalty
shoot-out. Ronaldo made his shot, which decided the
match. Then he tipped his head back and pointed toward
the sky. This one was for his dad. But Portugal did not
make it to the World Cup finals. France knocked the team
out in the semis. Germany took third place after defeating
Portugal 3–1.

A scuffle occurred between the English and Portuguese players during the quarterfinal. Rooney received a red card, removing him from the game, after an accidental foul on Ricardo Carvalho. Rooney told Ronaldo not to get involved. A misunderstanding caused the English fans to believe Ronaldo had a hand in Rooney's red card. Rooney and Ronaldo sorted the problem out themselves. But the English fans were not as forgiving. They went as far as posting comments online, telling Ronaldo not to return to Manchester. So, he didn't want to go back for the next season. Alex Ferguson and United's chief executive visited Ronaldo in Portugal over the summer and convinced him to return.

England football fans cheer for their team during a 2006 World Cup match in Germany.

When he got back to Manchester, Ronaldo dug in his heels and delivered for the team. He wrote, "Right from the beginning of the season I have tried to calm myself down and wear an icy mask during the games in which whistles abounded." Ferguson privately acknowledged his courage. He also told him that silencing his critics with his talent was the right approach.

## Becoming CR7

Ronaldo had planned to continue using the number 28, his number at Sporting, at Manchester. But Alex Ferguson had another number in mind. He told Ronaldo that he was going to wear number 7. Ronaldo agreed. Ferguson was his new boss after all. It took some time for the significance and honor of number 7 to sink in for Ronaldo. Manchester former greats George Best and David Beckham had worn it. Being given the number meant that the club had great expectations for him. He said, "This is in fact an iconic, historic number with enormous importance. It is an honor to have it on my shirt." Seven was also the number Luís Figo had worn for Portugal. Figo was one of Ronaldo's childhood heroes.

Ronaldo (*in the air*) scores a goal for Manchester United in a Champions League final against Chelsea in 2008.

Ronaldo's fourth season at United was his best yet. He received individual recognition for the first time in his professional career. In April 2007, he won the Professional Footballers' Association Player of the Year award. He also won the Young Player of the Year award. Both of these awards came from his peers who played for English and Welsh teams. He was the first player in 30 years to receive both in the same year. The last player to do this had been former Manchester United winger George Best.

The team also had a great season. United won
the Premier League for the first time in four years.
Ronaldo celebrated his first trophy. He could finally
feel what it was like to be a champion. He called it an
"unforgettable sensation."

In 2008 United claimed another Premier League
trophy. They also won Europe's Champions League for the
first time since 1999. Ronaldo was the top scorer in the
Premier League with 31 goals. His season total was 42.

In recognition of his individual achievements, he won
his first Ballon d'Or trophy by a landslide. This award
for best player is voted on by sports journalists. He
received 446 out of a possible 480 points and dedicated

Ronaldo shows off his first
Ballon d'Or trophy in 2008.

the win to his family, friends, and agent, Jorge Mendes. The following month, he took home the FIFA World Player of the Year award, chosen by team coaches and captains. Cristiano Ronaldo had become the world's best soccer player.

## COME ON, MADRID!

Spanish soccer team Real Madrid had been interested in acquiring Ronaldo, and he had publicly expressed interest in playing for them. Before the beginning of the 2009 season, the timing was finally right, and he joined the team.

Ronaldo plays for Real Madrid at a UEFA Champions League match in 2010.

Real Madrid paid Manchester United a record £80 million transfer fee, equal to about US $107.6 million. Ronaldo also became the world's most expensive soccer player. The news made headlines around the world. Ronaldo was joined by four other new players at Real Madrid. They were Kaka, Karim Benzema, Xabi Alonso, and Raul Albiol.

Real Madrid presented Ronaldo to its fans at Bernabéu
Stadium on July 6. Eager to meet the team's new star,
80,000 Real Madrid fans filled the Bernabéu to capacity.
They had been waiting in line much of the day to gain
entrance. Ronaldo wore a No. 9 jersey. Real Madrid's
legendary player Alfredo di Stéfano had worn that number.

During the ceremony, Ronaldo told them, "I have
made my childhood dream a reality, which was nothing
less than playing for Real Madrid. I didn't expect a jam-
packed stadium—this is truly impressive." Then he led
the crowd in a Real Madrid cheer. He shouted, "One, two,
three, come on, Madrid!" The whole stadium roared back

Ronaldo (*center*) fights for the ball with
players from Italian team AC Milan in 2010.

along with him. After an eventful day, he was officially on the team.

Ronaldo scored in each of his first four league matches during his first season. He was the first Real Madrid player to accomplish this feat. But he suffered an ankle injury during his second Champions League match in late September. Then he aggravated the injury while playing for Portugal the next month. He was out through the end of November.

Despite a long absence, Ronaldo was the team's highest goal scorer that season with 33 goals in all competitions. But the team didn't win a single title. Real Madrid lost everything to its rival and Lionel Messi's team, Barcelona. The overall results left Ronaldo feeling frustrated and sad. But the reality was that with so many new players, Real Madrid was not yet a cohesive team.

A joyous development in his personal life soon followed. In June Ronaldo became a father to a baby boy named Cristiano Jr. By agreement with the baby's mother, Ronaldo was his son's exclusive parent and guardian. The mother wanted her identity kept confidential. Ronaldo requested that everyone respect his right to privacy in this family matter.

The next season Ronaldo went back to wearing No. 7 when Real's team captain Raúl González Blanco retired. The team had a new coach, José Mourinho, and was winning again. Barcelona didn't take home all the titles this time. Real Madrid won the Copa del Rey, Spain's annual knockout soccer competition, for the first time in almost 20 years.

Ronaldo kicks the ball around with his son Cristiano Jr. in 2018.

In 2011–2012, Real Madrid faced Barcelona at Camp Nou for the league final and defeated its rival at home. Ronaldo was the only player in La Liga to have scored against all 19 other teams in a single season with 46 goals in total. But he wasn't the league's top scorer. Barcelona's Lionel Messi had 50 goals. But Ronaldo's third season at Madrid was his best yet, and his overall performance would keep improving.

# GOLDEN AGAIN

Ronaldo tore up the pitch early in the 2013–2014 season. He also renewed his contract with Real Madrid through 2018.

On September 6, Portugal defeated Northern Ireland in a World Cup qualifier. The match was Ronaldo's 100th for Portugal. A hat trick, or three goals in one game, brought his goal-scoring tally to 43. Eleven days later, he scored another hat trick against Istanbul's Galatasaray for Real Madrid. It contributed to a 6–1 victory. He had 66 goals in total for team and country in 2013.

He was once again contending for the Ballon d'Or in January 2014. His competition this time included Lionel Messi, who had won the previous four years, and Bayern Munich's Franck Ribéry. It was one of the closest contests in the award's history, but a clear winner emerged. Legendary player Pelé announced to the audience gathered at Zurich Convention Center that Ronaldo had won.

Cristiano Jr. attended the ceremony with him, along with other members of his family. His son joined him onstage, and Ronaldo was overcome with emotion. He thanked his teammates and family and shed joyous tears. Afterward, many people shared their congratulations. Runner-up Messi said, "Cristiano has had a great year and he deserves the prize." Portugal president Aníbal António Silva pointed out that Ronaldo was the first Portuguese player to win the award twice.

Ronaldo was suffering from injuries again in spring 2014. His doctors advised him to rest to prevent left leg problems from getting worse. In May Real Madrid was facing Atlético Madrid in the Champions League final. Real Madrid hadn't won the European Cup in 12 years. Ronaldo was determined to play despite his injuries.

Ronaldo risked further injury and played. His teammate Sergio Ramos's header put the game in overtime and enabled Real Madrid's win. The club was finally European champions again and had clinched its 10th cup, La Décima.

Ronaldo (*right*) battles Juventus player Leonardo Bonucci in a 2015 UEFA Champions League semifinal.

## La Décima



Within a year, Ronaldo's problem leg was finally better. At Euro 2016, Portugal reached the finals, which they had lost to Greece in 2004. This time, they played France, a tough rival.

Ronaldo was tackled early in the game and struggled to continue playing. Within 25 minutes, he was taken off the field on a stretcher. He turned his captain duties over to his teammate Nani. Ronaldo returned wearing sneakers and a knee support as the match was headed into overtime. From the sidelines, he and Portugal's coach, Fernando Santos, shouted at and encouraged the team until Eder scored in the 108th minute. It was a hard-won victory, but at last Ronaldo had won a major tournament for his country.

The following year brought another big development for Ronaldo's family. In June 2017, Eva and Mateo, his twin daughter and son, were born by surrogate in the

United States. A surrogate carries a pregnancy to birth
and then gives the child or children to their intended
families. He shared a picture of himself with his two new
children on Instagram and said, "So happy to be able
to hold the two new loves of my life." Just five months
later, another love arrived. He and his partner, Georgina
Rodriguez, whom he had met in 2016, welcomed daughter
Alana Martina to their growing family.

## GOAL MACHINE

Ronaldo had been with Real Madrid for nine years by
2018. The team had won the Champions League three
years in a row, 2016–2018. Although he had extended his
contract in 2016, he no longer felt essential to the club.
He was ready to leave and signed with Italy's Juventus.
Its fans had given him a standing ovation during a
Champions League match earlier that year.

When he left Real Madrid, he was its all-time highest
goal scorer with 451 goals in 438 matches. He had
surpassed the previous record of 323 in 2015. Juventus
was hoping Ronaldo would help them win the Champions
League. They had gone 22 years without winning.

During his first season, Ronaldo was once again
adapting to a new coach and teammates. The team got
knocked out in the Champions League quarterfinals.
But he helped Juventus win its Serie A league. Ronaldo
contributed significantly to the team's success by scoring

# World's Most Charitable Athlete

If there were a trophy for the athlete who's given back the most, Ronaldo could win that as easily as he wins soccer trophies. Much of his charitable giving and work has been for children. He's acted as an ambassador for several organizations, including Save the Children and UNICEF. The list of donations he has made throughout his career is long. In 2014 Ronaldo received a £450,000 ($576,284) bonus from winning the Champions League trophy. Instead of keeping it, he split it among three charities. When an earthquake hit Nepal in 2015, he gave £5 million ($6.4 million) to aid the country's recovery effort. He also donated €1 million ($1.1 million) to Portuguese hospitals during the COVID-19 pandemic.

or assisting in 40 percent of its goals. He became the first player to win league titles in England, Spain, and Italy. Juventus won its league again in 2020.

In September 2020, Ronaldo was playing in a World Cup qualifying match against Ireland. During that game, he scored his 110th and 111th international goals. He set a new record for the leading scorer in men's international soccer.

A Juventus victory in the Champions League hadn't come by the end of Ronaldo's third season. He was ready to move on. In late summer 2021, he returned to Manchester United, twelve years after leaving for Real Madrid.

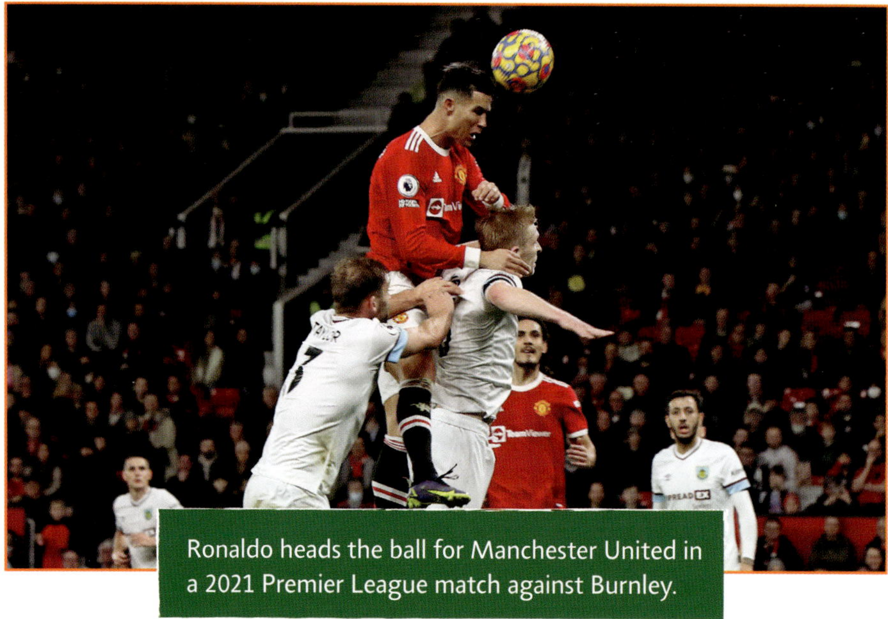

Ronaldo heads the ball for Manchester United in a 2021 Premier League match against Burnley.

Ronaldo's return to Manchester lasted just one full season. At the end of 2021–2022, United placed sixth in the Premier League and didn't qualify for the Champions League the next season. Agent Jorge Mendes sought a transfer for Ronaldo to a club competing in the Champions League, but none was forthcoming.

A bright spot for Ronaldo during a difficult year in his career was the arrival of his and Rodriguez's second biological child. Rodriguez gave birth to a baby girl named Bella. They were now a family of seven. But she had been expecting twins. Bella's twin brother died at birth. They named him Ángel.

During the following season with United, Ronaldo grew extremely unhappy with the coach and the team's owners. He wasn't grinning and bearing it, and his sportsmanship suffered. He left midgame during a match with the Tottenham Hotspur. He later apologized for his actions. But then he shared his frustrations about Manchester's management during a live television interview with British talk show host Piers Morgan. Soon after, he and the club reached a mutual agreement to terminate his contract.

Ronaldo became a free agent and headed to Saudi Arabia to play in the Saudi Pro League following the 2022 World Cup. Al Nassr signed Ronaldo in December 2022 for a two-year contract. Once Ronaldo made the move, other former Champions League stars followed. Karim Benzema went to Al Ittihad and Neymar to Al Hilal. In 2023 Ronaldo led Al Nassr to defeat rival Al Hilal 2–1 and claim its first Arab Club Champions Cup.

Ronaldo's legendary soccer career has been filled with highs and lows, trophies, awards, and many incredible on-field moments. He reached new heights of soccer success playing with Real Madrid, his childhood dream come true. He also made more history in men's international soccer in 2024. Ronaldo was not only its all-time leading scorer, but he made the most appearances—200 for Portugal.

Ronaldo's soccer legacy and longevity, his determination to succeed, athleticism, and generosity will be a source of inspiration for years to come. He's undoubtedly a superstar.

# IMPORTANT DATES

**1985**  Cristiano Ronaldo is born on February 5 in Funchal, Portugal, on the island of Madeira.

**1997**  He moves to Lisbon, Portugal, to train at Sporting Lisbon's youth academy.

**2002**  He makes his professional debut with Sporting Lisbon at the age of 17.

**2003**  He signs with Manchester United.

**2005**  Ronaldo's father, José Dinis Aveiro, dies in London.

**2008**  Ronaldo wins his first Ballon d'Or and FIFA World Player of the Year awards.

**2009**  He signs with Real Madrid.

**2010**  His son Cristiano Ronaldo Jr. is born.

**2015**  He becomes Real Madrid's all-time top scorer when he scores his 324th goal.

| | |
|---|---|
| **2017** | Twins Mateo and Eva are born in June. |
| | Ronaldo and partner Georgina Rodriguez welcome daughter Alana Martina in November. |
| **2018** | He signs with Juventus. |
| **2021** | He returns to Manchester United. |
| **2022** | Ronaldo and Rodriguez welcome daughter Bella. |
| | He signs with Al Nassr. |
| **2024** | He becomes the all-time leading scorer in men's international soccer. |

# SOURCE NOTES

12  Ben Hayward, "The 'Little Bee' Who Always Cried—The Story of Young Ronaldo's Path to Greatness in Madeira," Goal, September 29, 2023, https://www.goal.com/en-us/news/the-little-bee-who -always-cried-the-story-of-young-ronaldos-path-/k927thno26 e41b42er1z9zhqo.

12  Luca Caioli, *Ronaldo* (London: Icon Books, 2018), 6.

14  Caioli, 9.

16  Cristiano Ronaldo with Manuela Brandão, *Moments* (London: Macmillan, 2007), 54.

16  Ronaldo with Brandão, 52.

18  Cristiano Ronaldo, "Madrid: My Story," Players' Tribune, October 2, 2017, https://www.theplayerstribune.com/articles/cristiano -ronaldo-madrid-english.

20  Marcus Alves, "From the B Team to Man United: How Cristiano Ronaldo Broke Through at Sporting," Bleacher Report, May 14, 2020, https://bleacherreport.com/articles/2891112-from-the-b -team-to-man-united-how-cristiano-ronaldo-broke-through-at -sporting.

21  Gary Stonehouse, "The Real Deal Cristiano Ronaldo: Former Manchester United Star John O'Shea Reveals the Truth about Facing Portuguese Star," *Sun* (London), November 21, 2016, https://www.thesun.co.uk/sport/football/2233633/cristiano -ronaldo-former-manchester-united-star-john-oshea-reveals-the -truth-about-facing-portuguese-star/.

23  Alec Fenn, "Cristiano Ronaldo: Real Madrid Star's Journey to the Ballon d'Or," BBC, January 13, 2014, https://www.bbc.com/sport /football/25719657.

24   Ronaldo with Brandão, *Moments*, 136.

25   Ronaldo with Brandão, 100.

28   Ronaldo with Brandão, 167.

28   Ronaldo with Brandão, 83.

30   Ronaldo with Brandão, 173.

32   "Cristiano Ronaldo Welcomed by 80,000 Fans at Real Madrid Unveiling," *Guardian* (US edition), July 6, 2009, http://www.theguardian.com/football/2009/jul/06/cristiano-ronaldo-real-madrid-bernabeu.

32   "Christiano Ronaldo, 1, 2, 3, ¡Hala Madrid!," YouTube video, 0:37, posted by submarino87, July 7, 2009, https://www.youtube.com/watch?v=_38kUspPd0g.

35   Caioli, *Ronaldo*, 224.

38   Tanner Walters, "Cristiano Ronaldo Shares Photo of Newborn Twins," *Sports Illustrated*, June 29, 2017, https://www.si.com/soccer/2017/06/29/cristiano-ronaldo-twins-announcement.

# SELECTED BIBLIOGRAPHY


Alves, Marcus. "From the B Team to Man United: How Cristiano Ronaldo Broke Through at Sporting." Bleacher Report, May 14, 2020. https://bleacherreport.com/articles/2891112-from-the-b-team-to-man-united-how-cristiano-ronaldo-broke-through-at-sporting.

Begley, Emlyn. "Cristiano Ronaldo Breaks Men's International Scoring Record with 110th and 111th Goals." BBC, September 1, 2021. https://www.bbc.com/sport/football/58412201.

Caioli, Luca. *Ronaldo*. London: Icon Books, 2018.

"Cristiano Ronaldo Leaves Real Madrid to Sign with Juventus." *ESPN*, July 10, 2018. https://www.espn.com/soccer/story/_/id/37557982/cristiano-ronaldo-leaves-real-madrid-join-juventus.

"Cristiano Ronaldo: Top 10 Iconic Moments from His Career." BBC, August 31, 2021. https://www.bbc.com/sport/football/58383967.

Fenn, Alec. "Cristiano Ronaldo: Real Madrid Star's Journey to the Ballon d'Or." BBC, January 13, 2014. https://www.bbc.com/sport/football/25719657.

Marcotti, Gabriele. "Cristiano Ronaldo's Evolution as a Player: From Making It in Manchester to Madrid and Juve Goal Machine." *ESPN*, June 25, 2020. https://www.espn.com/soccer/story/_/id/37583983/making-manchester-madrid-juve-goal-machine.

Ronaldo, Cristiano. "Madrid: My Story." Player's Tribune, October 2, 2017. https://www.theplayerstribune.com/articles/cristiano-ronaldo-madrid-english.

Ronaldo, Cristiano, with Manuela Brandão. *Moments*. London: Macmillan, 2007.

# LEARN MORE


Britannica Kids: Cristiano Ronaldo
https://kids.britannica.com/kids/article/Cristiano-Ronaldo/633850

Jökulsson, Illugi. *Messi and Ronaldo: Who Is the Greatest?* New York: Abbeville, 2020.

Lowe, Alexander. *G.O.A.T. Soccer Strikers*. Minneapolis: Lerner Publications, 2022.

Messi vs Ronaldo
https://www.messivsronaldo.app

Nicks, Erin. *Cristiano Ronaldo*. Minneapolis: SportsZone, 2020.

Sports Reference: Cristiano Ronaldo
https://fbref.com/en/players/dea698d9/Cristiano-Ronaldo

# INDEX



# PHOTO ACKNOWLEDGMENTS


Image credits: Hokayem/Saudi Pro League via Getty Images, p. 2; Maciej Rogowski/SOPA Images/Sipa via AP Images, p. 6; Antonio Villalba/Real Madrid via Getty Images, p. 8; eye35.pix/Alamy, p. 9; ARCHIVIO GBB/Alamy, pp. 10, 14; PATRICIA DE MELO MOREIRA/AFP via Getty Images, p. 11; Valter Gouveia/NurPhoto SRL/Alamy, p. 13; Tom Brogan/Alamy, p. 15; ADRIAN DENNIS/AFP via Getty Images, p. 17; AP Photo/Paulo Duarte, p. 19; Helios de la Rubia/Real Madrid via Getty Images, p. 20; John Peters/Manchester United via Getty Images, p. 22; Serkan Hacioglu/dia images via Getty Images, p. 23; Professional Sport/Popperfoto via Getty Images, p. 24; Clive Mason/Getty Images, p. 26; Peter Macdiarmid/Getty Images, p. 27; AP Photo/Sergey Ponomarev, p. 29; AP Photo/Thibault Camus, p. 30; Jamie McDonald/Getty Images, p. 31; Jasper Juinen/Getty Images, p. 32; Pedro Fiúza/NurPhoto via Getty Images, p. 34; Denis Doyle - UEFA/UEFA via Getty Images, p. 36; Tom Purslow/Manchester United via Getty Images, p. 40.

Cover: Kazuki Oishi/Sipa USA/Sipa via AP Images.